WOMEN'S STRENGTH

Strong women don't play victims.Don't make them pitiful and don'point fingers. They stand and deal

Matthew T. McMillian

@ Copyright

Table of Contents

Chapter5:Challenging Gender Roles: Women in Leadership

Chapter: Indispensable Strength of Women

women's strength: breaking societal norms

Women's strength is often seen as an ability to break societal norms and challenge the status quo. Historically, women have been expected to conform to traditional gender roles, limiting their opportunities and potential. However, women's strength lies in their resilience

to overcome these limitations
and defy expectations.

One aspect of women's strength in breaking societal norms is their pursuit of education and careers. in the past, women were discouraged or even prohibited from pursuing higher education or entering certain professions. However, women have defied these societal expectations and now excel in various fields, including STEM, politics, and business. their determination to challenge the norm and achieve their goals demonstrates their strength and resilience.

Another arena where women showcase their strength in breaking societal norms is through advocacy for gender equality and women's rights. women have been at the forefront of historic movements such as suffrage, reproductive rights, and equal pay. They have faced criticism, discrimination, and even violence for their activism, yet they continue to fight for justice and equality. By challenging unequal power structures and advocating for change, women demonstrate exceptional strength and courage.

Moreover, women's strength lies in their ability to challenge and redefine societal expectations around appearance and body image. society often imposes unattainable beauty standards on women, creating pressure to conform and eroding their self-esteem. However, women have embraced body positivity and taken a stand against unrealistic beauty standards. They celebrate diverse body shapes, sizes, and appearances, promoting self-realization and confidence among women who, for too long, have been told they were limited or inferior.

The feminist movement has also highlighted the importance of individuality and self-expression for women. It encourages women to embrace their unique identities and make choices that align with their desires and values, free from societal pressure or expectations. This aspect of feminism has empowered women to reject traditional gender roles and define their paths in life, whether it be in relationships, family planning, or personal goals. By promoting self-realization and self-acceptance, feminism has helped women find fulfillment in being true to themselves.

Furthermore, the feminist movement has created spaces for women to come together and share their stories, experiences, and challenges. This has contributed to a collective realization that women's struggles are not isolated incidents but part of a broader system of inequality. By building solidarity and support networks, women can navigate the obstacles they face with a stronger sense of

self and a shared commitment
to creating change.

It is important to note that the feminist movement is not only about women's self-realization but also about creating a more equitable society for all genders. By advocating for intersectional feminism, the movement recognizes that different women face unique challenges based on their race, sexuality, socioeconomic status, disability, and other identities. Therefore, the rise of the feminist movement not only empowers individual women but also addresses the systemic barriers that hinder self-realization and equal opportunities for all.

In summary, the feminist movement has helped women embrace their strength, challenge societal norms, and assert their rights and worth. It has contributed to women's self-realization by promoting equality, individuality, and personal fulfillment. By creating spaces for dialogue and collective action, feminism has empowered women to recognize their capabilities, challenge existing power structures, and work towards a

more equitable and inclusive
society.

Rise of the Feminist Movement and Women's Self-Realization

The rise of the feminist movement has played a crucial role in women's self-realization and empowerment. Feminism advocates for gender equality and challenges the systemic oppression and discrimination that women have faced throughout history. This movement has encouraged women to question societal norms, redefine their roles, and discover their worth and potential.

One of the key aspects of the feminist movement is encouraging women to recognize their capabilities and pursue their dreams and ambitions. Feminism promotes the idea that women are just as capable as men in all areas of life, including education, career, politics, and leadership. By challenging stereotypes and advocating for equal opportunities, feminism has opened doors for women to explore their passions and achieve personal and professional success.

   This has led to increased self-realization and confidence among women who, for too long, have been told they were limited or inferior. The feminist movement has also highlighted the importance of individuality and self-expression for women. It encourages women to embrace their unique identities and make choices that align with their desires and values, free from societal pressure or expectations. This aspect of feminism has empowered women to reject traditional gender roles and define their paths in life, whether it be in relationships, family planning, or personal goals. By promoting self-realization and self-acceptance, feminism has helped women find fulfillment in being true to themselves.

Furthermore, the feminist movement has created spaces for women to come together and share their stories, experiences, and challenges. This has contributed to a collective realization that women's struggles are not isolated incidents but part of a broader system of inequality. By building solidarity and support networks, women can navigate the obstacles they face with a stronger sense of self and a shared commitment to creating change.

It is important to note that the feminist movement is not only about women's self-realization but also about creating a more equitable society for all genders. By advocating for intersectional feminism, the movement recognizes that different women face unique challenges based on their race, sexuality, socioeconomic status, disability, and other identities. Therefore, the rise of the feminist movement not only empowers individual women but also addresses the systemic barriers that hinder self-realization and equal opportunities for all. In summary, the feminist movement has helped women embrace their strength, challenge societal norms, and assert their rights and worth.

It has contributed to women's self-realization by promoting equality, individuality, and personal fulfillment. By creating spaces for dialogue and collective action, feminism has empowered women to recognize their capabilities, challenge existing power structures, and work towards a more equitable and inclusive society.

Facing and Overcoming Challenges

Facing and overcoming challenges is an essential part of personal growth and development. Here are some steps that can help in facing and overcoming challenges:

1. Recognize and accept the challenge: The first step is acknowledging and accepting

the existence of the challenge. Avoiding or denying it will only delay the process of overcoming it.

2. Analyze the challenge: Understand the nature, scope, and underlying causes of the challenge. Break it down into smaller, manageable parts to gain clarity and develop a strategy.

3. Develop a plan: Create a well-thought-out plan to tackle the challenge. Outline the steps and resources needed, set achievable goals, and create a timeline for completion.

4. Seek support: Don't hesitate to reach out to family, friends, or mentors for support. A fresh perspective or guidance from others can provide valuable insights and encouragement.

5. Take action: Begin executing your plan and take the necessary actions to overcome the challenge. Be persistent, adaptable, and stay focused on your goals.

6. Learn from setbacks: Challenges often come with setbacks and obstacles. It's important to learn from these experiences and adjust your approach as needed. Embrace failure as an opportunity to grow and improve.

7. Practice self-care: Taking care of your physical, mental, and emotional well-being is crucial during challenging times. Engage in activities that reduce stress, maintain a healthy lifestyle, and seek professional help if needed.

8. Stay positive and motivated: Maintain a positive mindset and cultivate a sense of motivation and resilience. Celebrate small victories along

the way to stay motivated and keep moving forward.

9. Reflect and learn: Once you have overcome the challenge, take time to reflect on what you have learned from the experience. Use this knowledge to grow and become better equipped to face future challenges.

Remember, everyone faces challenges at different points in life, and overcoming them requires patience, perseverance, and a willingness to learn and adapt.

The Strength of a Country: A Representation of Women

The representation of women in a country is a crucial indicator of its strength. When women are adequately represented in various spheres of society, it leads to a more inclusive, equitable, and prosperous nation. Here are

some ways in which the
representation of women
reflects the strength of a
country:

1. Political representation: A country that values the voices and perspectives of women in its political system demonstrates a commitment to gender equality. When women are actively involved in decision-making processes, they bring diverse viewpoints and experiences to the table, leading to more comprehensive and inclusive policies.

2. Economic participation: The participation of women in the workforce is essential for a strong economy. When women have equal access to education, employment opportunities, and leadership positions, it leads to increased productivity, innovation, and economic growth. Countries that promote gender equality in the workplace often have higher levels of economic development.

3. Education and health: The level of investment a country makes in the education and health of its women reflects its commitment to their well-being. When women have access to quality education and healthcare, they are better equipped to contribute to society and participate in decision-making processes. This not only benefits women but also the overall development of the country.

4. Safety and security: The safety and security of women are essential indicators of a country's strength. When women are protected from violence, harassment, and discrimination, they can fully participate in society and fulfill their potential. Countries that prioritize the safety of women demonstrate respect for human rights and the rule of law.

5. Cultural and social progress: A country that values and respects the cultural and social contributions of women fosters a more inclusive and diverse society. Recognizing and promoting women's achievements in areas such as arts, literature, sciences, and sports enriches the cultural fabric of a nation and helps challenge gender stereotypes.

6. Role models and inspiration: The visibility and recognition

of women in leadership positions and influential roles inspire future generations of women to aspire to greatness. When women can see themselves represented in diverse fields, it encourages them to dream big, overcome barriers, and strive for success.

In conclusion, the representation of women in various aspects of society is a powerful indicator of a country's strength. Governments, institutions, and individuals must work towards achieving gender equality and ensuring that women have equal opportunities to thrive. By creating a society that values and empowers women, nations can harness the full potential of all their citizens, leading to a stronger, more

inclusive, and prosperous
future.

Challenging Gender Roles: Women in Leadership

Challenging gender roles and roles and promoting women in leadership positions is essential for a more equitable and progressive society. Here are some reasons why women in leadership contribute to the growth and development of a country.

1. Diverse perspective: Women bring different experiences, ideas, and viewpoints to the decision-making table. By having more women in leadership roles' a country can benefit from a broader perspective, leading to more inclusive and comprehensive policies and strategies

2:Role model and inspiration: seeing women in a leadership position served as an inspiration to other women and young girls, encouraging them to pursue their goals and aspirations. Female leaders act as role models, breaking gender stereotypes and showing that women can excel in any field, shattering the glass ceiling and motivating others to strive for success.

3:Improve collaboration and teamwork: Women often possess strong interpersonal skills and inclusive leadership styles, which can contribute to better collaboration and teamwork. By promoting women into leadership positions, a country can foster a more cooperative and harmonious work environment, leading to increased productivity and efficiency.
4. Enhanced decision-making: Studies have shown that diverse teams, including

women, tend to make better decisions. Women are more risk-averse, cautious, and thoughtful in their decision-making process. By having women in leadership roles, countries can benefit from their analytical thinking, emotional intelligence, and ability to consider multiple perspectives in decision-making processes.

5. Addressing societal needs: Women, due to their unique experiences and challenges, may have an enhanced understanding of societal needs, especially in areas related to gender equality, healthcare, education, and social welfare. By involving women in leadership, a country can ensure that policies and strategies are developed to address these specific needs, leading to more effective and sustainable solutions.

6. Economic growth and competitiveness: There is a strong correlation between gender diversity in leadership and economic growth. Studies have shown that companies and organizations with diverse leadership teams tend to be more innovative, financially successful, and competitive. This principle applies to countries as well. By promoting women in leadership roles, countries can achieve economic growth and

maintain a competitive edge in the global arena.

7. Equal representation and democracy: In a truly democratic society, equal representation of women in leadership positions is crucial. It ensures that the voices and concerns of women are heard and considered in decision-making processes. By promoting gender equality in leadership, countries can demonstrate their commitment to democratic principles and fair representation of all citizens.

In conclusion, promoting
women in leadership roles
challenges traditional gender
roles and brings numerous
benefits to a country. By
providing equal opportunities
for women to excel and reach
leadership positions, countries
can foster more inclusive,
innovative, and prosperous
societies. It is crucial for
governments, organizations,
and individuals to actively
work towards breaking gender
barriers and promoting gender

equality in leadership for the benefit of all.

The Indispensable Strength women

The strength of women cannot be understated or overlooked. Women possess unique qualities and strengths that are vital to the progress and success of society. Here are some reasons why the strength of women is indispensable:
1. Resilience: Women have shown immense resilience in the face of adversity, overcoming obstacles and challenges with grace and

determination. They have demonstrated the ability to bounce back from setbacks and continue moving forward, often juggling multiple responsibilities and roles.

2. Empathy and compassion: Women tend to possess a natural sense of empathy and compassion towards others. They are often nurturing and caring, making them instrumental in building strong relationships and creating supportive communities. This empathy allows women to understand the needs and

concerns of others,
contributing to more inclusive
and compassionate decision-
making.

3. Emotional intelligence: Women often excel in emotional intelligence, which is an important leadership skill. Emotional intelligence includes self-awareness, empathy, and the ability to understand and manage one's emotions and the emotions of others. This skill allows women to effectively communicate, resolve conflicts, and build meaningful connections with others.

4. Collaboration and teamwork: Women are known for their ability to collaborate and work well in teams. They are often skilled at building consensus, finding common ground, and bringing people together. This collaborative nature helps to foster a sense of unity and cooperation, leading to more successful and productive outcomes.

5. Adaptability: Women have shown their ability to adapt and thrive in ever-

changing circumstances.
Whether it's managing work-
life balance, navigating
career transitions, or
adjusting to new
environments, women have
proven their ability to adapt
and find innovative solutions
to problems.

6. Problem-solving skills: Women possess strong analytical and problem-solving skills. They are often detail-oriented and can think critically and strategically. This skill set allows them to identify challenges, propose effective solutions, and drive positive change.

7. Intuition: Women have a natural intuition that often guides their decision-making. This instinct, combined with their analytical skills, enables them to make well-informed

decisions, even in complex or ambiguous situations.

8. Leadership style: Women often bring a distinct leadership style to the table. They are often known for their inclusive and participatory approach, listening to and valuing diverse perspectives. This leadership style encourages collaboration, fosters trust, and promotes a sense of belonging among team members. In conclusion, the indispensable strength of women lies in their

resilience, empathy, emotional intelligence, collaboration, adaptability, problem-solving skills, intuition, and unique leadership style. Recognizing and harnessing these strengths is vital for creating a more equitable, inclusive, and successful society. By valuing and empowering women, we can build a world that benefits from their many contributions and achievements.